OLD CODGER'S COOKBOOK

by
David Curwen

Illustrated by
Wendy McCleave

© 2013 The Executors of the Estate of David Curwen
© 2013 Drawings & Layout - Camden Miniature Steam Services

British Library Cataloguing-in-Publication-Data:
a catalogue record of this book is held by the British Library.

ISBN No. 978-1-909358-04-1

Also by David Curwen:
Rule of Thumb an Autobiography
Published 2008 Vintage Reprint Services

Layout by Andy Luckhurst - Trowbridge & Camden Studios

Printed by Imprint Design & Print
Newtown, Powys

Published in Great Britain by:
Camden Miniature Steam Services
Barrow Farm, Rode, Frome, Somerset. BA11 6PS
www.camdenmin.co.uk

Camden stock one of the widest selections of fine transportation,
engineering and other books; contact them at the above address for
a copy of their latest free Booklist.

TABLE OF CONTENTS

To an old Codger

Funneber ?

...hat is a Codger, a question I ask

...time and time again, and how man...

...d you have to have to your cree...

...on can really claim to have /min...

FOR AN OLD CODGER

What is a Codger? A question I ask myself time and time again, and how many summers do you have to have to your credit before you can really claim to have joined the club?

Of course there are Codgers and Codgers; Grumpy Codgers, Serious Codgers, and Happy-Go-Lucky Codgers. I hope I qualify for the last group, for if you are a grumpy old miserable one, you only upset other people, make yourself unhappy and other people do not really want to have much to do with you.

If you are a Serious Codger you have to find another Serious Codger with whom you can discuss all the serious things in life like politics, the weather, the state of the world and, of course, global warming, and fill yourself with fears of being drowned in a flood or scorched by the sun, stung by a mosquito (which I wish I could spell without having to look it up) and you go to bed wondering if you will wake up. That is if you managed to walk home safely in the dark.

But I find that a happy-go-lucky stand is a much better thing to have, you don't worry about what awful things are around the corner or what might happen. If there is a monster around the corner, or if a slate does slip off the roof and cut you in two, worry about it then, unless of course you are incapable of worrying about it, and in this case you can't worry can you?

Probably the best thing an Old Codger can do to join this band of H-G-Ls is to give a certain amount of attention to food and drink. They say, for instance, that you must drink at least eight cups full of liquid every day. How, I ask you? What is a cup full? A coffee cup? A tea cup small, a tea cup large or a ruddy great mug? I have a glass, it takes two tea cups small, one and a half large, so what? I am completely in the dark. Just drink enough so that you do not have to pay a visit to the smallest room when you have friends or are out at a party. It is so very embarrassing to have to ask your host "where is it?", and if she or he says "what?", you have to whisper and get looks, you know what I mean. But do drink; water, they tell me is a very good thing and it is just as good out of the tap as out of a bottle. Before we were on the mains, we had for many years our own well; much better, no chemicals you knew about and just the right amount of bugs, beetles and other bodies that gave it strength and flavour.

I have watched our cat and she much prefers the water in a puddle or in a bowl outside when the colour is murky or green than that clean water I put down for her. Mind you it must be in a large enough bowl, so that the sides do not touch her whiskers. Such is life.

We are rather straying from the point, which is easy food and drink, with H-G-L Codgers in view.

Before we leave drink, water is improved no end by the addition of a little whisky, or a lot if you have the money. Whisky is supposed to keep your blood thin, so it flows easily through your furring-up old arteries, and of course the Bible suggests a little red wine for your stomach's sake. White wine is pretty good too, and of course a Gin and

Tonic if you are thirsty; and a Gin and French or a mix if you need something that will bring your gout on; and if you need a pick me up Champagne and a spot of Brandy in it is fine; and if you have a tummy upset a mix of Port and Brandy is supposed to settle things, in any case it warms you up.

Now food - most important food, everything needs food, cats, dogs, horses and humans. If you are a H-G-L Codger you must have food and the following are easy recipes that you can do, without too much trouble and fairly quickly. If you don't know how to turn the electric cooker on, forget it, go and buy food from the nearest pub, but if you like having a go, cook something yourself. You may ruin the odd saucepan or frying pan but what does it matter? Plenty more in the shops. But of course it's a bit expensive, so don't put a red hot pan on the kitchen table or the sink top; you will be in terrible trouble and you might even catch the house on fire, make sure the firemen are not on strike and the fire station is not miles away. Of course buy a fire extinguisher, but if you have to use it, you may do more damage than the fire.

do everything without them, what have yo

Kitchen, I presume you have a kitchen?

have what is in it? and what is it

large or just a passage, in which if a

you have to squeeze by each other with

CHAPTER ONE

AN OLD CODGER'S CULINARY WORKSHOP

The most important thing in an H-G-L Codger's arsenal; your kitchen, you can't do anything without it. I presume you have a kitchen? And if you have what is in it? And what is it like? Small, large or just a passage, in which if a helper comes you have to squeeze by each other, or for the one nearest something hot or even boiling, a delicate part of one's body may get boiled, fried or otherwise mutilated.

Mine is rather small, if there are two of you in the kitchen you have to abide by traffic rules around the central table, no passing, you can't. I share it with the Cat and mouse and, at times, a small toad.

I think the mouse was brought in by the cat who managed to lose it and lost interest. She, the cat, is like me becoming an antique, so any extra effort just isn't worth it, but both mouse and toad may have come in through the cat's front door. I often wonder if our cats (we have always had a cat, all our lives), do they really appreciate how privileged they are? They live a life of complete luxury, all food found and if you are late - "where is it" meow; if she doesn't feel like coming down (she has taken over the bedroom) - "room service please"; if I wake in the early hours pat pat on me - "could I have a few biscuits please" and if you are going to read for a time - "please stroke my tummy, it's bliss".

They have their own room or hut built at vast cost onto the side of the kitchen, with their own tunnel into it in a 9" wall, with their own step up to it and an outside sliding door which I can close from inside. I like her in at night, too many Badgers etc. and of course the rain.

As you walk in from the dining room, straight in front of you is the sink, a three drawer unit I fitted years ago. I had a new stainless steel sink fitted and later 2 lever taps, because these were easier for my wife who had bad arthritis. I had lever taps fitted throughout the house, except the spare room, for the same reason, they are very good. Now back to the kitchen; to the right of the sink there is a sliding door, at least it was sliding, it was also a mistake. Old cottages are like old bones, the weather affects them, they move and sliding becomes jamming, an extra heave is required, so have ordinary doors with gaps.

When I put on a small extension years ago, the youthful inspector of work made us put in two-foot deep foundations. I told him and pointed out to him that the cottage has no foundations, built on the earth 300 or more years ago and still here (at the time of writing that is). It made no difference, it was the law, so now we have at least a small part with a foundation.

Now if you can manage to get through the said sliding door, there is a small cupboard-like area, full of junk, the waste bin, shelves with

things that might come in useful, next week's dustbin or, as they say, recyclables; papers, bottles - far too many of these, but why not? There is the back door on the left; this was not there when we bought the cottage. Most important there is a special hole in the wall for Mistress Quickly, the cat, where she can get into a specially built wooden room for cat trays, emergency only, she prefers the outside for this job. She runs the house.

(There has been a gap of several months just at this point, I'm glad to get back into writing again. Do you get gaps? First this, then that, the odd dose of flu, only the odd one mind.)

The drains - I've always hated drains. Filthy smelly drains, but we can't do without them. Although I seem to have managed the major part of the last war with that wonderful invention, The Elsan; 'orrible, just 'orrible, doesn't deserve an 'H'.

Well, back to the kitchen, if you walk straight ahead, leave the aforementioned 'sliding' door on the right, in front of you is the sink in a sink unit that was bought from a firm in Bath and brought home lashed or crammed into the VW Beetle we had then. Now, like me, it has seen better days. A little maintenance would have helped, but being a good engineer you don't waste time maintaining anything, you just wait 'till it breaks down and it takes hours and hours to repair. One of the drawers has far too many kitchen tools - knives, forks, spoons, ladles; careful how you put your hands in or you may have to wave a finger ta-ta.

The cupboard under the sink beggars description; powders, fluids, dustbin liners, large saucepans for boiling ham. As long as you open the doors carefully OK, otherwise you may have to spend the next hour cleaning it up and putting things back. Next to the sink is the washing machine, new two years ago, and now, as a widower, I have to work it. Good as long as you push the right buttons and put the washing powder in. The previous washer - I suppose it was our first - was expensive and very, very good, but like me it passed its three score years

ago and at times it would walk a bit and had to be put back an inch or two. When on spin I liked to leave the room just in case, you know. Of course the time came when pushing the button on it just made a rather offensive noise and nothing more. Eventually Tony was called, the man for the job, and I saw him start to remove miles of wire and little bits, the names of which I didn't know. He told me "sorry the programme has gone" and it's too old to get a new one.

Programme? I thought that was a thing you bought in the theatre.

Anyhow, the only thing to do was to buy another and, with tears, send the dear old machine down to the scrap heap. Now the new one, you can hardly hear it washing. Of course it was not made in Britain, nothing is made here these days. Except the vast profit the dealers make by buying cheap and selling to us, the gullible Briton, for a great deal more. What will happen when the makers are no longer content with a bowl of rice a day? Try and guess …

Now, over the magnificent machine is a shelf, as I put it up it's wonderful - it has stayed up; shelves are not my favourite things. On this shelf is a small dishwasher, 4 or 6 person only, no room in the inn for a full-size one.

Now I have great respect for this little machine, we share views on life. We, neither of us like to be watched while we are working. I cannot bear being watched, it gives me the gebbies, so much so that I manage to hit my thumb or finger with the hammer or pinch it with something, pliers or so. Now this machine is the same, you must load it up, put in the powder, turn it on and go out of the room as soon as possible, then, in about an hour, everything is done and spotlessly clean.

Fiddle with any of the switches trying to hurry things up and you are in deep trouble. I did this one day, came back and it had stopped half way through and nothing I could do; trying switching this and that and it would not start. Ah, think I, a fuse - take the plug out, unscrew it, drop the screw, of course, put in a new fuse, grovel on the floor and at last find the screw. OK try again …nothing, not a tick or a squeak. So it must be a main fuse - which is the main fuse, there are stacks of main fuses in my fuse cupboard? But, after many minutes trying this and then that, I find it, it's OK. So what, it still doesn't work, shall I call the repair man? Well I better have a look at the instruction book; when I finally manage to understand the book, it says that the machine will cut out if it overheats. Open the door of the machine and the back door, so you freeze, and after a few minutes try again and yipee everything is fine. Silly, silly me, I hope you do something silly at some time, if you don't you have not lived, and if you do, and do not laugh at yourself, you have not lived at all.

Move onto the next machine, close up to the little dishwasher - the microwave. Now there are many who say "wouldn't have one of those". Hang on a minute, just hang on, listen to how a microwave actually works. As an engineer I came across the principle years ago, they found that induction heating metals for treatment, hardening etc. could be done more evenly and with less mess than with flames and furnaces. It worked through a system of coils of wire passing a current through them, which heated things from the inside out, rather than flames that heated from the outside inwards.

This is why there are millions of meals served in restaurants and pubs, with very few cases of food poisoning. Most bugs get well inside, so if you heat food from the inside till it is hot outside, it no longer has semi-hot insides full of bugs. Q.E.D and your microwave will heat food safely.

So there it is, and it's quick for an Old Codger. However, I have to refer to the instruction book all the time as I refuse to fill my memory store with things the book will store for me. When you think about how much you store in one small head, well it just is not worth thinking about.

Oh, by the way, if you have some nice plates or dishes with silver or gold decorations on them, do not put them in the microwave to heat a meal up. Metal is taboo, you will get sparks, flashes and what not, and all the sweet designs will just disappear - I know, I have dun 'un.

Next is the electric cooker, this uses far more expensive electricity than the microwave, which on the highest setting is 800w. Your cooker can use 9k.w all on, and individual rings are probably 2 or 3 k.w. each.

When we first came to the cottage (actually I should say, after we were married), we had a gas cooker, but the cottage - or village for that matter - had no gas, so we brought a good British-made Belling cooker, very up to date, rows of dials and timers, so that you could put your meal in, go to church or a party after switching it on, come back and hey-presto all done. Hey-presto mine was not even hot, so I gave the automatics up.

This state of affairs lasted many years, up until the time I had to take things apart and fit new switches more and more frequently. So the time had come and with a mental tear or two a new cooker took its place. Have you noticed that every time you replace an old faithful, its descendant is of far less quality than its ancestor? You may not have noticed, as you are probably not as far past your "sell by" date as I am. Well the new Belling came, poorer quality for more money. This goes for everything, light switches were nice ceramic one with strong springs on and off. No sir, out of date, EU regulations: "you must have our neat plastic switches, much better". Don't be kidded.

Well the new Belling was OK but, as my wife's health was getting bad, more and more of the cooking came onto me. Well, I like cooking, but the 'phone would go at the wrong moment, or I would think it would take some time to boil, so I have time to do so and so; alas and alack the burnt meals and the demise of saucepans was great and with this cooker, spillage went through the rings to inaccessible places, most difficult if not impossible to clean.

So in a rash moment, I spent a vast sum on a cooker with a ceramic top. If it boiled over now, it could not go through. Hurray! However, my pleasure was short lived, it couldn't go through but it could cook itself hard on the ceramic top and be careful, you must not scratch it. So it became, the opposite of a labour of love, whatever that may be, to clean it and use the "special" cleaning fluid only supplied by Belling. Belling again, buy a good British make. Oh yes, until the stove arrives in its large cardboard box, with where it was actually made written all over it.

I hope you can cope with a fan oven, so far either the chicken is underdone, or cremated, but I may learn as time goes by. It does, doesn't it? Despite its drawbacks, the fan makes a lovely noise when on, lovely until you can't stand it anymore.

Now you are in a corner, the remains of the base of the old copper chimney, now bricked up and of course tiled in elegant blue, false Copenhagen tiles. This chimney that was contains all the cooker and other electric switches, pity it's such a business moving all the bits and bottles before you reach them.

We have turned a right angle, - I suppose it is such, I've never checked it - and now we face a long shelf under a window, a good spot for the odd wasp to sun itself, not many this year. Here is the toaster and electric kettle. Of course the kettle is as far away from the water tap as can be, but it's one that parts company with its bottom, so you are able to spill water all over the electrics if you don't watch out. This of course puts all the lights out, that is if you have a proper safety trip switch. It is very necessary, but very trying! I've just had a new one fitted, the electrician said you just flip the cover open and press the button twice. Just try flipping the cover open with a torch in one hand; took ten minutes at least, and now I've forgotten what on earth I did! By the way always have a torch handy; you know just where it is, oh bother I had it somewhere else, where? But we have finished with the kettle, so there is just the toaster. When crumbs dribble out of the bottom it is time to clean it.

Now the rest of the shelf, oh dear the rest of the shelf! All the little bottles, peppers, salts and what have you - you can lose anything here. But it is light, there is a window looking out onto the drive, which you can hardly see for some nice bushes and a nice yellow rose. Mind you, on the windowsill there are a few things that can block the light; a slow cooker, a mixer, electric of course, must have one, useful for whipping things up - things like white of egg, advanced cooking this, a pretty chopping board, never used, far too pretty, a flour dispenser, like a large pepper pot, you only have to shake it and flour flies everywhere, including over you, watch it. Next another electric mixer, I think this comes under the title of liquidiser, very very useful for soup making and turning anything you are wearing, a nice white shirt or apron into an artist's impressionist painting. Next the herb cabinet on the wall, two compartments, open the outside door and there are shelves full of little bottles of herbs etc, close this door and there is a clip, clip it and open again and there are deeper shelves on which you keep sugar packets and many other packets. Do, do be careful how you pull these doors open, a jerk and you can have a major disaster. On the door of this cabinet is an electric clock, if I remember correctly a free gift many years ago from someone we dealt with, but it works, now and again needing a small battery.

Now turn once more to the last wall leading to the door you came in, work surface, cupboards, two drawers, two cupboards underneath, full to overflowing with treasures. You can't use the top as a work surface, it has a bread maker, some cook books and other items such as a radio. On the wall above, a cupboard with crockery - how it manages to hold all that china is a miracle and long may it stay a miracle. Between this and the corner of the room is a shelf, with more cookbooks than you can ever need, including several many years old, our first cook book nearly 60 years old now, and two much older books, my late wife's mother's book and an old Mrs Beeton.

Next to the cupboards and the door, the fridge and freezer, God bless them, without them life would be much more difficult. These two items must be as close as possible or you can't open the kitchen door, but that is my problem.

In the middle of all this, a kitchen table, small but with two flaps - just room for you to get around - and of course stools etc. crammed under. That is it. No more for a time, Cat must have its supper, she sits on the back of an easy chair near the door, this means "have you forgotten the time?"

Now here is a small appendix, about the aforementioned slow cooker. I thought that an appendix was a part of your body, the Almighty gave you by mistake, and you can let your surgeon remove it without much harm. Jacky, she is my niece - no, really a niece, not the sort of "niece" many old men have. Well Jacky came along with a hefty parcel,

"you need one of these".

"what?"

Oh, a "slow cooker".

"What do I need this for?",

"Well did you not say you have a bit of a job with hard food having lost those little bits of ivory in your mouth many years ago?"

True, very true, I have little bits of plastic which work at half cock. How much plastic do I have at 97? Teeth, eyes (cataract), ears - one in each, tummy - oh yes a plastic bag. Heart still goes on pumping, how many times in 97 years? Must be getting a bit tired.

life time, and now after m

you find that there was a

has to trained his staff,

always find a welcome a

and such pleasant service

CHAPTER TWO

AN OLD CODGER'S MATERIALS

Now the most important thing is to have a good supplier and in this I really have one and to him I dedicate this book. We have dealt with Rose & Son, butchers of Devizes for over 50 years now. The business was owned by a Mr and Mrs Cartwright when we first came to All Cannings, a village about 6 miles east of Devizes, under the Downs in the Vale of Pewsey.

Mr and Mrs Cartwright are still with us, they live in a farmhouse near the monument in the Nursteed Road out of Devizes.

Mrs Cartwright always rang us up on a Thursday or Friday for our order and it always finished, by "and what about something for the Pussy?" Most important, a little bit of rabbit! How did old Tom know that Friday afternoon was delivery day? He would, without fail, wait on the shelf by the back door, to make sure the delivery was made. Tom had the extra sense that animals have in a very great degree. I was often away on business and my wife said that she knew when I was on my way back, as he would wait outside the front of the house for my return. If we had been away for a few days, we always called for a cup of tea at my in-laws' house, Rose Cottage, and while we were there Tom would come down two or three hundred yards and cry outside for us.

He knew or the fairies told him, but his extra sensory perception was very advanced.

When you get a change of neighbour or, for that matter, someone you deal with such as a purveyor of first class meat and game, one always has terrible qualms of "what on earth will they be like? The worst of these, in days gone by, was one's Bank Manager; was he going to squeeze you or would he become a friend, most important?

So far, and it's now too late to worry about all these things, the Gods have been more than generous to me. Our cottage in Wiltshire is close by the old Rectory, we share the drive with them. In 1951, when we brought the two cottages, which were in a terrible state, nearly being allowed to fall down, they were owned by a farmer, but before this - many years ago - had been the Gardeners' and Coachmens' cottages for the Rectory, when Rectors had coachmen, the Rector at one time usually being the youngest member of a noble Family.

At the time we bought the cottages, the Rector and his wife were from days now past, visiting the Parish sick each afternoon. When they left we had another four Rectors and families staying a few years, and moving on, then about 25 years ago the church sold the Rectory to a private owner and, about 10 years ago, it changed hands again due to death. Each time it was a worry, who would come? What would they be like?

Well, after 10 years they became good friends and wonderful neighbours; you would have to hunt the country from top to bottom to find better. Being carted off to hospital at 11.00pm in an ambulance, Rosie insisted on coming, and stayed till 3.30 in the morning until all my tests and X-rays were done, and Rosie is the sort of person who made sure there was little delay.

Yet again we are straying a little away from the main purpose of this epistle, which is of course Cooking for Codgers, and in this at last we come to the major person in all this - Stephen Cook. When the

Cartwrights finally retired, Stephen Cook, whose family already had a very good butcher shop in Devizes, took over Roses. What now? Would we get the same service from our butcher? What was Stephen Cook like? No need, no need at all to have worried; the service continued and over the years one begins to realise there was just a bit more, and now after many years you find that there was a lot, lot more. He has so trained his staff that you always find a welcome smile and such pleasant service it would be impossible to better. I want to find an excuse to visit his shop, much as it would be better for my purse if I had not, but still you can 'phone and get a feeling that they like to talk to you. And Stephen, just a supplier of high quality food? No, a friend, someone who will always do one a favour. As an old one, it is not always possible to get into Devizes to buy the odd thing from Sainsburys, such as a bottle of the hard stuff, so very, very necessary for a man who is now long past his sell by date.

No problem, he will always help, in fact on the 'phone with one's weekly or fortnightly order, his staff say, "anything from Sainsburys, Mr Curwen?". A very good friend, and a person who likes a good Jaguar too; I have a 37 year old one.

...eeings of a lemon, the skin if

drop or two of juice if you can't.

Put the salmon fillet skin side

a piece of foil, on an oven t

buas from mixture, well into

CHAPTER THREE

THE RECIPES

We had better cut out the preliminaries and get down to the main purpose of this book - cooking, easy cooking, no worry at all. Most quick meals as described in recipes are far too complicated, so in this case you will need to use your grey matter to fill in the gaps, but keep your grey matter in its proper place.

Firstly, unless you like to think about your coming meal, I recommend a glass of whisky, whichever type you favour - or wine - and a little something to go with it. At Roses delicatessen you can get many pleasant things, but you may have to put your fingers deep down into your purse or pocket. There are delights such as large olives in several styles, small strips of salmon in sauce, prawns and many other things. There is also a selection of cheeses which I dare not look at, or I will come out loaded with parcels and so very much poorer. So, I order on the 'phone, and if I am feeling mean I buy some pigs liver; carefully fried and cut into small strips or little blocks, it goes very well with a drink. However, don't forget the cocktail sticks, sharpened up matches are a bit off and unless you smoke, you may not have matches in the house. I don't think I have any. What do you want to strike a match for anyway?

In the following pages you will find recipes for:

SOUP

Tomato
Carrot
Pea
Artichoke

FISH

Game Fish: Salmon and Trout
Haddock
Scallops
Kipper
Flat Fish

MEAT

Beef
Pork
Veal
Venison

POULTRY

Chicken
Pheasant

VEGETABLES

SOUPS

I suppose soup should be the first thing on the menu; there are many different soups, it's all a matter of stewing things up and in many cases adding the odd leftover you think might help. An egg cup full of sherry always helps, if the soup is a bit poor, more than an egg cup for shure. (You need not put the "H" in sure unless you are putting in more than an egg cup).

Unless you are thinking of boiling up old bones and the like, meat, leftovers and such, a very good tomato soup is very simple, and a good starting point

TOMATO SOUP

Ingredients:

- 1 tin chopped tomatoes
- Butter
- Chicken stock: homemade or from stock cube
- Salt and Pepper
- Basil: chopped leaves or dried Basil
- Onion
- Salt & Pepper
- Orange juice
- Sugar

Tomato Soup - making:

Get a tin of chopped tomatoes or any other tinned tomatoes and an onion. Skin and dice the onion, put it in a medium-sized saucepan with a nugget of butter and fry until soft - not brown and crisp, oh no, just soft. Oh, by the way, don't forget to turn the gas or electric oven on. Open the tin of tomatoes and tip them in. Next make a pint to ¾ of a pint of stock from a chicken cube, or of course if you are foolish enough to have stewed your last chicken carcase into stock, use this. I find making stock from old bones and carcases is a bit of a bore, as I am inclined to forget them until the house is full of the pungent fumes of the pot boiling dry; my turnover of cremated pots is much heavier than should be.

Now, back to the soup. Put in the stock, a little pepper and salt, an egg cup full of orange juice if you have any, a teaspoon of sugar, bring to the boil and simmer for 10 minutes or more. Just as you are about to serve, put in a good dose of chopped Basil leaves or a good teaspoon of dried Basil. Plus sherry to taste.

A good soup, easy to make, but with real tomatoes and not tinned tomato soup which can only have glimpsed a tomato on the table. Maybe it was only told about real tomatoes.

CARROT SOUP

Ingredients:

- Carrots
- Orange juice
- Flour
- Lea and Perrins Worcestershire Sauce
- Sherry

Carrot Soup - making:

This is just about the same as tomato. Cut the carrots small or slice them into strips using a slicer - mind your fingers, spoils the flavour if blood and finger is added. Don't worry about the onion, a little orange juice, a tablespoon or so, and if you want it thick, a tablespoon of flour mixed in water just to a roux, add to the carrot and bring to the boil to thicken. If you wish to give the soup a bit of a kick, some Lea and Perrins Worcestershire Sauce helps and don't forget the pepper and salt to your taste. Once the carrots are stewed you can also add the odd left over you think might help.

PEA SOUP - INGREDIENTS:

Ingredients:

- Peas
- Half Pint Vegetable or Chicken Stock
- Mint or Mint Sauce

Pea Soup - making:

Again this soup uses a similar methodology to tomato soup. Put a drained tin of peas into a saucepan, add ½ a pint of stock and bring to the boil. For any soup, the best stock is either vegetable or chicken. Add some mint to the soup, or even add mint sauce. You can then thicken the soup up, as you do for carrot.

ARTICHOKE SOUP

Ingredients:

- Artichoke
- Milk
- Parsley
- Salt and Pepper
- Potato
- Butter
- Stock (fresh or from cube)

Artichoke Soup - making:

Now this is a soup, provided you are on your own, or with friends who understand, if you know what I mean! In an ancient book I have it refers to Jerusalem Artichoke as being 'somewhat "windy meat", it produces "the lust"'. I don't think lust meant the same then as now.

Skin the artichokes, give them a quick boil up (this removes some of the gas-making effects), tip this water away, add more water, add a medium to large potato, and now cook until soft, again tip this water away. Mash them up with butter and add half a pint of milk and half a pint of stock, mix to a soup consistency. Warm through slowly, add some parsley, and as for any soup, add salt and pepper to your taste, and you have a soup for Royalty.

LEFTOVERS:

        - Chicken Breast
        - Butter
        - Olive oil
        - Left over soup of choice

Now here is another little dish I've just found out. If you find the soup is thick or if you have a little left over, thicken it by simmering it and put to one side. Buy a chicken breast, cut it into cubes about an inch square - all right, all right - 25mm x 25mm if you must be a heathen. Cook this in a pan or frying pan in some butter or olive oil, doesn't take long. NO metric time yet, thank goodness. If you cut a chunk in half with your scissors, it should be white right through, no pink bits as before you cut it up. Now just put it in the thick soup and heat them up together. OK, done.

Remember to wash your scissors well, never take liberties with chicken or it will take liberties with you; always cook well and hot.

OLD CODGER'S ADVICE:

Just a word about pots, frying pans etc.. I have tried for years not to do what I always do with dire results; put something on to heat up or boil, and think 'that will take a few minutes to boil, I'll just go and do some task or look for something while it does...', fatal, oh calamity, calamity, you get interested in something, or the 'phone rings and if the steam does not reach you, maybe the smell or stink does, and you rush out and alack and alas, oh dear, there are a few little silver shiny bits in the flour by the cooker.

I did not know some thick bottoms of some pans were stuck on with something like silver solder; now I do know, they are, and there is a round burnt place on the wooden dustbin cover outside, where my late wife dashed out with a very, very hot empty pan.

One learns, I don't!

Thank goodness the kettle and the microwave switch themselves off.

FISH

Now the next thing is fish. 'Make haste' as the politicians say, there won't be any left soon. But, as you have probably gathered, politicians keep what brains they have in their feet and the only use they have for their heads is to talk a lot of rubbish. Anything they are plugging, like global warming for instance, is always pushed out in large portions. But then the experts and scientists are called in when they have something to hide and want us, who they think are the stupid public, to forget about the mess they have made, usually a war they have got the country into.

As usual we have deviated from the point, the point being fish. Fish - well as you know there are little fish and big fish, nice fish and fish just longing to gobble you up if you are not looking, or if you are for that matter. I'm just going to deal with the fish most codgers love to gobble up themselves.

GAME FISH:

- Fillet of Salmon or Trout
- Butter
- Breadcrumbs
- Parmesan Cheese
- Basil
- Herbs
- Salt and Pepper
- Lemon Shavings (unwaxed) or Lemon Juice

SALMON AND TROUT:

Game fish, why game? I suppose it is because these are the favourite fish for the fly fisherman, once the sport for wealthy gentlemen, now for those who can pay for the sport. What is so nice is that, of late, most of these sportsmen only take a fish they want to eat; if they have enough, or the catch isn't big enough, they use hooks and bring their catch to the net, remove the hook and return the fish carefully to the water, none the worse for its experience except a small prick.

So now pay your fishmonger a visit and get a Salmon or Trout fillet, size to your liking. I don't know your appetite off hand, I usually have one about 1½ inches across. (Do you want it in millimetres? If so it's about 36, 40 if you are hungry.) You can also fillet your own Trout, as usually they are sold whole. Freeze what you don't use immediately

In a saucepan, put a knob of butter to melt. Now here is another difficulty, what is a knob? It could be so small you have a job to get it between your fingers, or it could be so large you find it hard to get it in your hand. So I suggest about the size of a walnut. When the butter is melted, remove from the heat and into it put enough breadcrumbs to cover the flesh all over, about ¼ inch thick or more. Add a dessert spoon full of parmesan cheese, some Basil, herbs, pepper and salt as required, and some shavings of a lemon, the skin if you can, a drop or two of juice if you can't.

Get a nice piece of aluminium foil, oil it a little on one side, put on an oven tray and place the fillet skin side down on this. Press your breadcrumbs mixture well into the top of the Salmon. Now 10 or 12 minutes in the oven at 180 degrees centigrade and, hey presto, it's done. If a little white milky fluid is coming out of the fish it's definitely done, but make sure not to let the crumbs burn.

SALMON RAMEKINS:

- Tinned Salmon
- ½ Pint White Sauce
- 2 Tablespoons of Cream
- Salt and Pepper
- Hard boiled Egg

Here is one more which can be a main meal or in small bowls or ramekins as starters. I use a tin of salmon as the main ingredient, although you could probably use fresh if cooked again.

Mix the fish together with ½ pint of white sauce, 2 tablespoons of cream, and salt and pepper. Mash some spuds and hard boil an egg. Put the mashed spuds around the edge of the dish or small bowl, pour the mix into the centre and garnish with the sliced egg. A good, quick, easy meal.

HADDOCK:

       - Smoked Haddock
       - Onion
       - 1 Tin of Chopped Tomatoes

or

       - Smoked Haddock
       - Butter
       - Plain Flour
       - Milk
       - Salt and Pepper
       - 1 Ounce of grated Cheese
       - Tomato
       - Breadcrumbs

There are two easy dishes made from Smoked Haddock. Again for both a slab thereof is needed from the fishmonger, or fish counter, either deep or lightly coloured.

The first is easy, just lay your Haddock flat on your aluminium foil or in a baking tray. Cut an onion into rings or small pieces, put this on top, open a tin of tomatoes - not plum, chopped, with or without herbs and pour ½ a large tin over the top (use the rest for a little soup), then place in the oven at 180 - 190c for about 20 minutes, don't overcook.

The second dish requires a tad more effort. First you must remove the skin. You may have better means of removing the skin than I, my way you must watch it a bit or you will get cremated fish, not eatable fish. To remove the skin, put it skin side up under your grill (it would be a good idea to put it on a piece of foil in a tin pan, or you will get the smell of burning fish in the kitchen for several days).

As soon as the skin begins to brown and blister it is quite easy to remove it from the fish. Probably best to wrap the skin and bones in plastic and put it in the dustbin. If your cat is anything like my friend, it turns its nose up at leftovers, nothing but the best.

Contd. over

Now all you have to do is flake the fish, break it up into pieces if you prefer, and put the flakes into a pie dish, remove any bones, but leave just one to choke on, adds to the fun.

In a saucepan make a roux. (What a silly French word for a mess of bits.) You require a knob of butter, an ounce each of flour and cheese and half a pint of milk. Melt butter, add flour and stir them up into a good paste and add milk slowly, stirring it in so there are no lumps. Add salt and pepper to taste and ½ an ounce or more of the cheese and mix up well. Pour over the fish, sprinkle with the rest of the cheese and if you have a few tomatoes quarter them and stick them around. I like to sprinkle some breadcrumbs with a few strips of butter on top.

Hey presto, into the oven at 180c until well bubbling and browning a little. A good easy meal to which it is a good idea to add slices of hard boiled eggs; goes further!

SCALLOPS:

- 2 or 4 Scallops
- Olive Oil
- Butter
- Salt and Pepper
- Buttered Toast

All depends on how deep is your purse? Not my business of course, but if you really like shellfish have a go, and just have one less glass of the hard stuff, two make a starter, four a light meal. These days with everything else tits up, there are so many cooking programmes on TV that things are TVd just to make them different, don't be fooled or you will loose the flavour of the real thing.

Scallops just need frying in olive oil and butter with salt and pepper to taste. Get the oil and butter good and hot, pop the scallops in for a few seconds on one side, and over to the other to seal the juices in. Then cook one side till it's just brown all over and then do the other side the same. Have a piece of well-buttered toast on hand, plonk the Scallops on, add a little parsley if you like and get eating.

KIPPERS:

....

    - Kippers
    - Salt and Pepper

I like kippers from time to time, not as much as a friend of mine who always has kippers and champagne on his wedding anniversary. I find it best to buy a Manx Kipper.

These can be cooked by just plunging them into a saucepan of boiling water for a few minutes, but personally I like mine a little cremated. Lay the kippers meat side up, flat out on aluminium foil, a large enough piece to fold over, with no gaps, parcel like, put it on a baking tray and under the grill at about 190c (after many years complaining I have had to go metric). Go away, have a drink and in 20 to 30 minutes it should be done.

You can take them out from time to time to see if they are done. Keep them closed as much as possible or you will get your leave stopped for smelling the house out. If you live in a flat, don't be surprised if you hear a hammering on your door. All you can possibly do is say "I'm so sorry I can't smell anything", and if you really don't like your neighbour or even a friend, see if you can manage to get his car bonnet open and put a piece on his exhaust manifold. Heresy.

To save washing up, I just open up the foil which I put on a large plate, and eat it from there, with plenty of pepper. Doing it this way, all the leftovers, bones etc can be rolled up in the foil and dumped into whatever you dump things in; if you are lucky enough to still have an old wife, not in her lap please.........

FLAT FISH:

- Brown Sole or Lemon Sole
- Butter
- Salt and Pepper
- Chopped Parsley

Flat fish, those you don't see till you have trodden on them, that is if you are at the seaside. Don't, for Codger's sake, tread on them in the fishmongers, he and his customers might become unfriendly.

Brown Sole, I will not say anything about them, or not much, as I'm sure you cannot afford them and Lemon Sole is almost the same. Why it's called Lemon, goodness knows, but then why are you called Jack or John or David? Maybe your old mother knew why.

The Bear in Devizes Market Place, when I used to go there in the 1950s, was kept by a chap who rejoiced in the name of Arthur Earl. He had been in charge of Churchill's Club in London, why he came to Devizes only he could tell you, maybe the peace and quiet, let's not get into it.

He used to serve the largest Brown Soles in his restaurant that I have ever seen. They overhung the plate and they were good, the memory of them makes my mouth water. I was having dinner there one night with my old friend, Mr Hancock, and at the next table was H.R.H Prince Charles with some officers, I think, all just incognito; no fuss, peaceful meal, can't quite make out if it was a case of him doing me the honour of his presence or me doing him the honour of mine, but I think it must be the first.

Can't think of a better way of cooking flat fish than to smother them in butter, a little pepper and salt, and grill them both sides, not for long, don't overcook fish. The exact cooking time depends on the size of the beast, anything from 2 to 5 minutes per side - if you can get just a little brown crispness that's well and good - add a little finely chopped

Parsley on top. If you want vegetables, chips, mashed potatoes and peas, OK, but just a little bread and butter - this is fine.

OLD CODGER'S ADVICE:

I think this about covers fish, there are many wonderful fish in the seas. Enjoy them, but don't get too close, remember Jonah, he didn't do what he was told to do. I wonder if he wasn't very good flavour and the whale was very pleased to get rid of him.

MEAT

I suppose we ought to get onto meat, unless of course you are a vegetarian, if you are you should not be reading this book, definitely not.

A good source of proteins meat is, whatever proteins are. Most necessary they say. Why? I've never worried if I had enough protein, vitamin C, D, F or X and somehow I am still with you all at 97, few blips at times, but nothing to worry about too much.

Meat, well meat; the first in the forefront of a good Englishman's mind is beef. If you don't like beef, I am afraid there is something wrong, you may need treatment from a trick cyclist (psychologist). Beef can be had in so many forms to suit you all.

Mind you, there is something of the savage, ancient Brit in me. I come from a brigand family, 1000 years or more in the north, Cumberland, Westmorland, now called "Cumbria. Why"? What's wrong with Cumberland or Westmorland? Anyhow beef for my ancestors was much cheaper than you get from Roses - if they didn't mind risking life or limb, my ancestors just nipped over the border and snaffled a beast or two from the Scots. Maybe you had to shed a drop of blood, preferably Scots blood, but it was worth it, what was left over from the feast you had was passed on to the locals and you became the hero, the benefactor. Curwens were loved, but not on the other side of the border, I fear.

ROAST BEEF:

- 2lbs or more Beef
- Salt and Pepper
- Any extra fat provided.
- Potatoes and Vegetables
- Yorkshire Puddings

Beef can of course be cooked in many ways, I present to you H-G-L Codgers two of my favourites!

Roast Beef of Old England, you can't beat it, a really nice piece of topside, Rib, Sirloin is wonderful. Some like it well done, I think it's best very red with good red gravy, roast potatoes, Yorkshire pudding. The only thing here is that you must have at least 2lbs of meat to get the real good flavours. So you have to make up your mind, can I stick beef in various forms for a week or so? Or freeze a bit for a later date? Don't do what I do and forget to label it. You come weeks later, pull something out, what the hell is this? Oh well, I suppose it's OK, it usually is.

Roast your beef, preferably in an open roasting dish, tin, aluminium or glazed earthenware. Sides help to stop any fat splatter in your nice clean oven, if you have such a thing. Or, if you want to be extra careful, put it - the meat I mean - in a roasting bag, supposed to keep the juices in, but doesn't brown the outside so well. Whichever way you choose give it a good dose of salt and pepper, and if your butcher has put a slice of fat on top, put it on top. Depending on how you like your beef give it plenty of heat, say about 15 minutes to each pound at 190-200, Gas 5-6 for pink in the middle or 10 minutes per pound for red in the middle, but watch it, as ovens vary. When you take the meat out of the oven, cover it with foil and let it rest for 10 minutes.

Whilst the joint is taking life easy, you can add roast potatoes and greens, such as brussel sprouts, and if you can make Yorkshire Puds that is fine. If you can't, you can get Yorkshire Puds from your supermarket, Aunt Bessie's Yorkshire Puds are best, all ready to put in the oven. By the way, take it out of the packet first, if you don't you will impair the flavour somewhat.

For the best roast potatoes, I like King Edwards or Maris Piper. It depends on the joint's size, but you will amost certainly have to put the potatoes in the oven before the joint.

Peel the potatoes and cut them into chunks - the smaller the chunks, the quicker they cook. Put a glug of oil, or a chunk of goose fat, in a roasting tin and put it on the top shelf of the pre-heated oven to get very hot. Put the cut-up potatoes in a saucepan with cold water covering them, bring to the boil for 5-6 minutes. Drain the potatoes into a colander, then return them to the saucepan, now dry from its own heat. Give the potatoes a shake to roughen their edges, dry cook for a minute or two - this makes a mess of the pan, but the result is worth it.

Remove the now very hot roasting tin from the oven, and spoon the potatoes on to it. The fat will spit and make a mess, but then you cannot make omelettes without cracking eggs; silly saying, but it seems apt! Back in the oven for 30 minutes or so. Remove the tray a few times, turning the potatoes over. Best to use tongs for this. Back in to the oven until they are golden and crunchy. Try to time all this so that they finish off whilst the meat is resting.

BEEF STEW WITH PIGEON:

- Beef
- Pigeons - 2 breasts
- Bacon
- Stock
- Onions, Mushrooms & Carrots
- Mixed Herbs

Now here is another one, just done it funnily enough. If there is only one of you, half the amount will do, but I do the whole lot so that I can get about three meals out of it. Don't have it day after day, gets boring, so have it first hot, next day something else, cold next, then something else, and if you can't stand it again, put curry powder in; how much? Well how hot do you want it? I take it you have a fridge, always use a fridge...... Oh yes the method, the modus operandi or something.

One, get a couple of Pigeons, butchers usually have them; these days they cost more than the 2/6d they did, probably a quid plus. All ready to cook, of course, feathers all gone and insides also. But perhaps if you have a gun, live out in the sticks and a farmer friend lets you be brutal, you can get your own. Personally I think a quid is cheap, my memory of W.W.2 shooting for meat, I hated the plucking and then de-gutting, a bit squeamish.

So get your pigeon breasts, 1lb of stewing steak and some mushrooms, onions, butter etc. If you have a metal or china casserole dish OK, if you haven't, use a frying pan or wok with a lid.

Put the pigeon breasts in your chosen vessel, add bacon (chopped in to small pieces), then the breast, cut in to cubes. If you are worried about wielding a knife or kitchen scissors to do this, the butcher will be pleased to. Add the chopped onions, carrots, mushrooms and seasoning. Half fill the dish with stock and add mixed herbs. Cook gently for 3 hours at 160-180, 3-4 gas. To boost the end result, add a wine glass of dry red wine about half way through cooking. If cooking for a dinner party, best not to add the rest of the bottle to yourself.

PORK:

. . . .

- Pork Fillet
- Olive Oil
- Herbs: Rosemary, Marjoram, Lemon Thyme, Tarragon
- Salt and Pepper
- Lemon Juice

Pork, an easy one, get a pork fillet, you know what that is, it's an elephantine sausage of pork, probably the most expensive cut. Do the sealing bit, hot oil in a frying pan, fry pork in both sides 'till it's well scorched.

But first, I should have said, get a large piece of aluminium foil, large enough to completely parcel the fillet, rub it all over with oil, olive oil for preference, not motor oil, or paraffin, they have far too strong a flavour.

Add a few herbs, rosemary, marjoram, lemon thyme and tarragon. I use thyme, I don't know what the lemon part is. Marjoram, well what the hell is marjoram? A herb, you can buy it in little bottles in the supermarket. Rosemary, well that's different, there is a rhyme, when "rosemary thrives the woman she drives". It thrives very well here, even though my poor wife is no longer with me.

Put all these herbs, plus salt and pepper to taste on the foil, and put the scorched pork on top, but don't cremate it, better not fry it at all than cremate it.

Now the next most important thing, a good large tablespoon of lemon juice over the fillet, this takes the oily fillet and makes it lovely. Put it in the oven at about 180c for 35 minutes. Oh by the way, fold up the aluminium foil so as little as possible of the steam can escape, before you put it in, not after.

VEAL:

- Thin Slices of Veal
- Breadcrumbs
- Butter

Now Veal, I find it best as nice thin slices with breadcrumbs rubbed in. You fry these in butter, not too long each side, say 2 minutes each side if it's thin. Lovely.

I feel I ought to eat veal. Why? Well you see farmers have to have calves for their milk, in this country they are kindly killed; kill them kindly, don't let them be sold abroad. So eat plenty of veal.

I'm not doing too well at the moment, very much like my 38 year old Jaguar. I need a certain amount of spirit to keep all cylinders going up and down. I'm not sure of the M.P.G for the Jaguar right now, but I think she uses a lot more than my malt!

VENISON:

- 1 or 2 Venison Steaks or Escallops
- Salt and Pepper
- Crushed Juniper Berries
- Olive Oil

Venison, why do I like it? First, because I am a bit squeamish (had to look this up in the dictionary!) about the killing of animals. Difficult isn't it? I love meat: dead animals!!! I believe I have been told by a friend who worked on a deer farm, how they were killed (I hate the word slaughtered). A licensed man kills a deer by a night shot, no hassle, one moment the selected deer is alive, the next he is dead; he doesn't feel anything, no terror, no long trip to a slaughter house. If we like meat, this is the kindest way to get it. Possibly game; hares, rabbits and game birds, are shot the same, so I like game in all its forms.

A great benefit of venison is that it is the healthiest of British animal meats, being low in bad fats - something that you have to remember when cooking it.

Now Venison, well if there is only one of you or perhaps two, venison steaks or escallops are possibly best. These just need salt and pepper rubbed in and, most important, crushed juniper berries pressed well in. Now don't overcook, a couples of minutes each side under a hot grill or in an oiled frying pan, I like it quite rare. You can cook it more if you like, but don't make it a cremated brick.

Another way is to use Venison snippets which make a good stew very much like beef.

...get you pigeons, get 1 lb of ste...

...some mushrooms, butter etc

...you have a metal casserol o.k.

...use a frying pan or wok ...

...you earthenware or china casse...

POULTRY

ROAST CHICKEN:

....

- Whole Chicken
- Butter
- Salt and Pepper

Chicken is good roasted whole. Put them in an oven tray on aluminium foil if you like, smooth butter all over them, sprinkle pepper and salt to your taste and pop them in the oven at 190, gas mark 5, depending on the size, for 45-60 minutes (20 minutes per pound), nice to get the skin a bit crisp. With chicken, stick a fork, or something pointed, in a fat part near a bone; if any red fluid comes out, it needs more cooking, any fluid should be clear. Rest the bird for 15 minutes before carving.

CHICKEN WITH HONEY
AND MUSTARD SAUCE:

- Chicken Breasts or Portions e.g. Wings
- 1½ Teaspoons of Honey
- 1 Teaspoon of Whole Grain Mustard
- ½ Teaspoon of Tarragon
- 1 Tablespoon Tomato Puree
- ¼ Pint of Chicken Stock from Stock Cube
- 1 Tablespoon of Cornflower
- Salt and Pepper

Either get chicken breasts or some chicken portions from your butchers, I always have the wing portion. Put your chosen cut into a casserole dish.

In a bowl mix 1½ teaspoons of honey, 1 teaspoon of whole grain mustard, ½ teaspoon of tarragon, 1 tablespoon of tomato puree, ¼ pint of chicken stock (cube), salt and pepper and add a tablespoon of cornflour mixed to a paste with water.

Pour all this gunge over the chicken and give it 20-25 minutes in your microwave at medium heat (70 or 80%). Turn the chicken over a couple of times, so it gets thoroughly coated. This is a good meal hot or cold, when the gunge becomes like jelly.

OLD CODGER'S ADVICE: CHICKEN SOUP

Now when you have had a hot, and possibly several cold meals from it and you are getting a bit fed up with chicken, remove all the flesh off the carcass and cut it into bite-size or smaller bits. Put them in a saucepan and cover with a tin of mushroom or chicken soup and heat up. Make sure you do this for long enough to thoroughly heat through the meat, if you prefer heat the meat first in olive oil, but not too much or it may get hard.

PHEASANT:

- Whole Pheasant
- Butter
- Olive Oil
- Grapes or Raisins
- One or Two Sausages

Birds that fly, Pheasants are one of my favourites, not only are they beautiful when alive, they also make a wonderful meal when they are dead and well cooked.

Well no bother about this, roast is the only way. Smother it with butter or oil of the olive, butter I prefer. If you like, stuff it with grapes or raisins, gives it a wine flavour. Stick it in the oven at 200c for 10 minutes, then about 180c for 45 to 60 minutes. Cooking time depends if it is young or old, how do you tell? I don't know, it's too late to ask it. Oh by the way, if you have a sausage or two, put them round the sides.

It's also a good idea to smother some olive oil, not too much, over the pan, saves a lot of scraping and swearing when you have to clean up after.

a couple of shallots, cut up so you he

ips and put into butter in a frying pa

potatoe slices and fry up till just bro

n can do this with Rosemary in p

onions/ by the way don't forget to s

VEGETABLES

Now I suppose with all these recipes we should think a little bit about vegetables. Vegetables, why vegetables? I don't know, but all the "must do this" health merchants make a play of vegetables.

NEW POTATOES:

- New Potatoes
- Butter
- Salt and Pepper
- Sprig of Mint Leaves

Potatoes:

Now everyone thinks first of potatoes, pomme de terre. Who the hell brought this soggy lump to this country? Walter Raleigh? Well, he also brought tobacco so that cancels it out.

& New Potatoes:

Once upon a time the first New Potatoes in the spring were quite something, they still are if you grow them yourself like Norman Blake of All Cannings. But the supermarket ones, oh dear. Some years ago, I think it was in Budgens, before they became Sainsburys, I was about to buy a few new spuds and noticed that they were from Egypt. There was an old dear about to do the same, she said to me, "I wonder what these are like?," and that dreadful quirk of fun in my mind led me astray. "Well madam", said I, "I should think they are pretty good, but mind you wash them well". "Oh why?" she said, "well madam it's nearly all sand in Egypt, so the only way they can get such good potatoes is to use what camels do naturally". "Oh dear", she said, "I see what you mean, perhaps I'll leave them until the Jersey ones come along". Goodbye and thank you. Well they don't have Camels in Jersey - cows of course, and maybe still earth closets. Most supermarket vegetables are of necessity grown for quantity and not flavour; the nurseryman must earn a living.

You don't always have to boil new spuds. Try washing them, then get a piece of aluminium foil large enough to make a completely closed parcel. Put in a lump of butter, rub the potatoes in it a bit, add salt and pepper and a good sprig of leaves of mint, fold up tight and put it in the oven at about 180c (Gas mark 4) or with what you are roasting. Time depends on the size of the potatoes - check after 20 minutes or so, taking care when opening the foil.

MASHED POTATOES:

- Potatoes
- Salt and Pepper
- 2 Teaspoons of Salad Dressing
- Hard Boiled Egg

Now my possible favourite, good mashed potatoes. Have you got a peeler? Rather like a very small version of a catapult or a Jews Harp. (You know, a plastic U with a handle underneath and a sort of blade joining the two arms.) So, to get on with the job, wash the potatoes clean, hold firmly in one hand so that you have the longest side exposed and pull the cutter across this. The more pressure the deeper the cut, and do be careful, please do be careful not to stroke the cutter over your fingers and hand. Slices of human skin and foreign bodies are not a good idea, even if they come from a non-foreign source and if your mash comes out pink, all you can say is, "I put a little Tomato Ketchup in for flavour". Liar.

When all the skin is off the potato, cut into slices, they boil so much quicker. When soft, drain and add a lump of butter, salt and pepper and mash with a fork or better still a masher. For flavour I add a couple of teaspoons or so of Heinz (or any other) salad dressing. If you are doing enough for 4 people you can make them Duchesse by adding one egg, (please take it out of its shell, unless you are a bird and need grit for your crop), a dollop of butter and cream. Mix together, leaving the surface with ridges. If you are only doing enough for 2 a whole egg is too much, unless you like mushy mash.

LYONNAISE POTATOES:

- Potatoes
- 1 Small Onion or 2 Shallots
- Butter
- Rosemary
- Salt and Pepper

You can of course do potatoes in many different ways. If you like onions, try Lyonnaise: Par boil the potatoes, what the hell par boil means, why not say part boil, or cook them but not quite? Wash but don't peel yet, and boil in salted water till they are beginning to soften a bit, testing with your prodder. Drain, skin and slice into slices a bit less than ½ inch. Skin a small onion or a couple of shallots, cut up so you have some strips and put into butter in a frying pan. Add the potato slices and fry up till just browning, you can do this with rosemary in place of onions. By the way don't forget to add salt and pepper to them to your liking.

PEAS:

- Peas
- Butter
- Mint

Peas, God bless them, the best without a doubt are those you pick in pods in your own garden, but you do need a lot of pods to get a good meal. They, like all veg, need to be cooked before they start to wilt, in other words as soon as you can. The flavour is superb; mind you, you should discard the odd wiggly white maggot. If you fail to, no matter, it will add to the protein or something, as long as you don't see it.

Of all frozen veg, peas are by far the best and you would need a vast quantity of pods to make a packet as per Mr Birds Eye. I haven't found a bad one yet, so they must have used a lot of spraying to stop the little maggots getting in. Or do you suppose the little packaging machine has a special maggot magnet to catch them all as they go by?

I like mint on peas, easy to grow - too easy in fact, it spreads everywhere. The other advantage to frozen peas is that Mr Birds Eye, or whoever you prefer, informs you of the correct cooking method, and the correct timing.

CARROTS:

- Carrots
- Butter
- Pinch of Sugar
- Mint
- Raisins

Carrots, well you know those long round red things or they can be round I think. Buy them from a shop, nice, clean, no holes, all probably due to chemical sprays. Grow them yourself, nice, very nice when young, when older, the odd bug has probably had a nibble first.

After scraping, you can just slice them or I prefer to cut into matchstick pieces. Boil until tender, drain well and put a bit of butter in the pan and a pinch of sugar and wiggle them about a bit and heat up again. You can try flavouring with mint or with some raisins, makes you see in the dark perhaps.

ARTICHOKES:

- Jerusalem Artichokes
- Lemon Juice

ARTICHOKE

- Cheese Sauce
- Walnut Oil or Butter

Now here is a veg you may and you may not like - the Jerusalem Artichoke. They grow like sunflowers, but only sometime have small yellow flowers, you find them best after a frost. They are all knobs and wrinkles, but if you grow them you will find they are prolific, so you can cut the knobs off and they will grow if planted.

There are several ways of cooking artichokes. After you have removed the skin, boil until soft. Oh by the way, when you slice them put 'em in water with a little lemon juice, or they go grey. Now artichokes are a bit like boiled spuds, you can put them in a pie dish, cover with cheese sauce and it's "au gratin". Why the French? In our native tongue "in cheese sauce".

Another good way of cooking: after peeling, cut into slices and boil till soft. Drain well and mash them, using some walnut oil if you have some, otherwise use butter.

But now comes the rub, you may like them, they may not entirely like you, so take them easy. I love them a little at a time. I cannot do better than quote from an 1814 Culpeper book I happen to have:

"They are under the dominion of Venus and therefore it is no marvel if they provoke lust as indeed they do, being something windy meat". I do not think lust meant in 1814 just what it means today, maybe it does, but "windy" they certainly are - a friend calls them "Cracker

Jacks" - but they have a lovely sweet flavour.

Mind you, this is if, and a second if, you like a lovely sweet flavour - you may not. The last people I gave a few to, all complete peeled and cooked by me, all they said was that 'it wasn't quite a flavour they liked'. So I should lay off artichokes if I were you, they are only for crazies like me.

OLD CODGER'S ADVICE:

How do you tell when potatoes are soft? Pinch one of the old lady's knitting needles, plastic covered for choice, stick one end into a cork (if you haven't got one have some wine!). With this you can test the softness of your potatoes - stick the pointed end in the potato and, if it slides out easily, your tatties are done.

An Old Codger's Farewell

Now I have written enough, far too much in fact, so just have a go, but mind the back of your hands and your fingers. When you put them in the grill - ouch it don't 'arf burn.

Good luck, happy edible meals.

AFTERWORD FOR THE COOK BOOK

My uncle, David Curwen was a great cook - I got all my best recipes from him ! He was about eighty when my aunt became seriously ill, and he said to me that if he wanted to eat, he had to learn to cook. This he proceeded to do with his usual aplomb - using a series of very elderly cook-books and his tried and tested "Rule of Thumb" method. If the prescribed ingredient was not available (even from the famous Roses of Devizes) he would substitute something else - occasionally with interesting results. And all washed down with a hefty draught of whisky.

A great friend of his started making his own bread - I gave David a bread maker, and he was away ! The same thing happened with the slow cooker! As a lifelong engineer, he loved machines, and even well into his nineties was never afraid to try something new.

This cook book came about because he felt there might be other old codgers about having to learn to cook at a late stage in their lives, and ever the practical man he thought others might benefit from his experiences. If you have enjoyed this book, you will have a flavour of my uncle - he wrote as he spoke, straightforwardly, unpretentiously and with a great deal of humour. I miss him a great deal, but you only have to open this book, and there he is.

Jacky Barnes (his favourite niece he said - actually his only niece ! But he really was my favourite uncle.)

Wendy McCleave

Wendy McCleave studied art at Farnham College of Art and University College, Falmouth. She works in a variety of mediums but focuses mainly on acrylics and charcoal. Her favourite subjects are life drawing and painting, and buildings and structures in the landscape, the more quirky and weathered the better; beach huts feature strongly. She undertakes commissions and may be contacted through her website: **www.beachhutart.com** where you will also find more examples of her work.

To her regret, Wendy never met David Curwen, although she was able to visit his cottage, and all the interior and exterior drawings in this book are of this.

Walter Rose and Son

This excellent butchers will be found at:
21-22 Sidmouth Street,
Devizes,
Wiltshire,
SN10 1LD
Tel: 01380 722335
www.walterroseand son.co.uk

David Curwen died, aged 97, in May 2011 shortly after handing over his beautifully handwritten text for this book, telling us 'to publish it if we thought it worthwhile'...................